WHAT IS 1?

Dr. Troy Shepherd, OCT, PhD

What is 1?
Copyright © 2024 by Dr. Troy Shepherd, OCT, PhD

All rights reserved. No part of this publication may be reproduced, distributed, or transmitted in any form or by any means, including photocopying, recording, or other electronic or mechanical methods, without the prior written permission of the author, except in the case of brief quotations embodied in critical reviews and certain other non-commercial uses permitted by copyright law.

Tellwell Talent
www.tellwell.ca

ISBN
978-1-77962-414-7 (Paperback)
978-1-83438-965-3 (eBook)

Dedication

This book is dedicated to all children and all inner children. May your imagination continue to be unlimited.

Acknowledgement

I would like to thank Elder Heidi McBratney, for your outstanding mentorship. To my mom, Louise Borrice Cummings, thank you for dreaming me into being and encouraging me to dream. To my sister Cherry-Anne Shepherd, thank you for believing in me. To my brother Otis Borrice, thank you for the fun we had together. To the Elders, Thomas Eldridge, the late Malidoma Somé, Mandaza Kandemwa - thank you for seeing my gifts. To the children and inner children who have taught and continue to teach me - thank you!

One is made of many.

Many can be one.

One can be any,

One is the Earth.

One is the Sun.

One is even a walk or a run.

One is a mystery. We use it to count.

Then we know how many,

or measure amount.

One is a finger, or even a pair.

We count 1 to make it fair.

One is a mystery, it cannot be heard.

1 = One

It can be a numeral or even a word.

One is a dot.

One is a place.

One is everything in time and space.

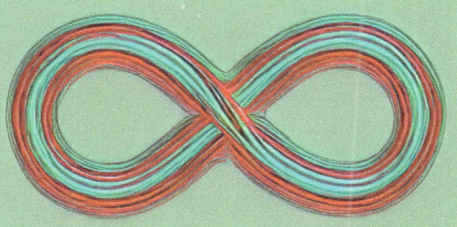

One is a person, place or thing.

One is a song that everyone can sing.

One is a dog.
One is your pet.

One is together with the whole planet.

One is togetherness. One is glue.

One is even a reflection of you

One never began and will never end.

One can be anything including your friend.

One is a whole.
One is a part.
One is in math and 1 is in art.

- WHOLE: 1 entire pizza

- PART: 1 slice (one part)

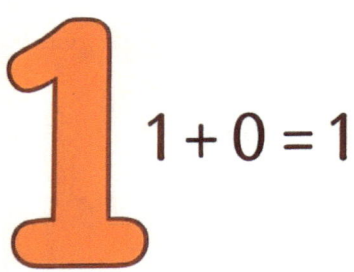

- MATH: the number 1

- ART: 1 flower (one art piece)

Lesson Plan Math and Art

Lesson Plan: Understand the Counting Principles of Abstracting and Unitizing

Grade Level: K-6

Subjects: Mathematics, Art

Lesson Objective

Students will:

1. Understand the concepts of abstracting and unitizing from an axiometaphorical perspective.
2. Develop flexibility in thinking about the number 1 and its representation in various contexts.

Materials Needed

*

Drawing and colouring materials

*

A set of cut-out geometric shapes (e.g., squares, circles, triangles)

*

Storybook What is 1?

Read the book What is 1?

Discuss Unitizing (5 Minutes)

Activity: Unitizing with Real-Life Examples

*

Hold up two fingers like a peace sign and ask, "How many?"

* *

Students may reply: "Two."

*

Say, "Yes, and it can also be 1 peace sign. Three fingers could be 1 triplet, four could be 1 quartet, and so on."

Key Teaching Point:

Explain, "Unitizing means grouping items together to create 1 unit. Any number of things can make 1 group, like one peace sign or 1 class of students.."

Abstracting Activity (5 Minutes)

Draw a square on the board and ask, "How many are there?"

*

Students reply: "One."

*

Ask, "One what?"

**

Students reply: "One square."

*

Draw a square and a circle. Ask the same question: "How many?"

**

Students reply: "Two."

*

Follow up: "Two what?"

* *

Guide them to answer: "Two shapes."

*

Draw a square, a circle and a pencil. Ask, "How many?"

* *

Use wait time for answers. Accept reasonable responses like "Three things"

Key Teaching Point:

Explain, "Abstracting means we can represent anything with the same number because we are focusing on the quantity, not the specific type."

Hands-On Practice (10 Minutes)

Activity: 'Abstract' Art

*

Ask students to draw or paint 3 different objects. They then exchange with a partner and try to categorize each other's items and name the category.

Reflection and Closing (5 Minutes)

Reflection Questions:

1. How did the "Abstract" Art activity help you understand the concept of abstracting?
2. Can you give an example from your everyday life where you use unitizing?
3. What was the most surprising thing you learned about the number "1" from this lesson?

Assessment

* Observe students' participation in discussions and activities.

* Review their artistic representations and categorizations to ensure understanding.

* Use their responses to reflection questions to assess their grasp of abstracting and unitizing.

For more, visit www.mathematizingspirit.com

About the Author

Troy Shepherd, OCT, PhD is a teacher, author and consultant. He has earned bachelor's degrees in science, commerce and education. He has also earned master's and PhD degrees in education from the University of Toronto. After a calling to be initiated and trained as a shaman, Troy embarked on a journey to reconcile his scientific and spiritual selves. His research involves mathematizing spirit so that students can create complementarity between their scientific and spiritual selves.

Visit Troy online at www.mathematizingspirit.com.

www.ingramcontent.com/pod-product-compliance
Lightning Source LLC
LaVergne TN
LVHW071653060526
838200LV00029B/448